Suzuki®

GUITAR SCHOOL

Volume 1
Ensemble Guitar Parts for Suzuki® Guitar School
Arranged by Simon Salz
International Edition

MW00396401

CONTENTS

Introduction 2

1 **Twinkle Ensemble,** *Folk Song* 3

2 **Lightly Row Ensemble,** *Folk Song* 6

3 **Go Tell Aunt Rhody,** *Folk Song* 12

4 **Song of the Wind Canon,** *Folk Song* 19

5 **May Song Ensemble,** *Folk Song* 22

6 **Allegretto Ensemble,** *S. Suzuki* 28

7 **Perpetual Motion Ensemble,** *S. Suzuki* 31

AMPV: 1.01

© Copyright 2022, 1996 International Suzuki Association
Sole publisher for the entire world except Japan: Summy-Birchard, Inc.
Exclusive print rights administered by Alfred Music
All rights reserved. Printed in USA.

ISBN-10: 0-87487-928-0
ISBN-13: 978-0-87487-928-5

INTRODUCTION

The purpose of these arrangements is to provide a variety of interesting and challenging reading material for Suzuki guitar students who are beyond Book 1 and are playing in a Suzuki guitar group class. These arrangements allow for students, who may be widely divergent in playing levels, the opportunity to perform together in the Book 1 repertoire. These arrangements include: the original melodies transposed one octave higher, giving the student practice in reading ledger lines and playing beyond the 12th fret; an obbligato melody that poses technical challenges to advanced students; a simple chordal accompaniment that gives Book 2 students excellent free-stroke arpeggio practice; and a bass part that gives the student practice in reading the lower ledger lines. These parts work well together but can also be used alone with the original melodies.

Twinkle Ensemble

Folk Song
Arr. S. Salz

Twinkle Ensemble

Guitar I

Folk Song
Arr. S. Salz

Twinkle Ensemble

Guitar II

Folk Song
Arr. S. Salz

0928

Twinkle Ensemble

Guitar III

Folk Song
Arr. S. Salz

Twinkle Ensemble

Guitar IV

Folk Song
Arr. S. Salz

0928

Lightly Row Ensemble

Folk Song
Arr. S. Salz

0928

Lightly Row Ensemble

Guitar I

Folk Song
Arr. S. Salz

Lightly Row Ensemble

Guitar II

Folk Song
Arr. S. Salz

0928

Lightly Row Ensemble

Guitar III

Folk Song
Arr. S. Salz

Lightly Row Ensemble

Guitar IV

Folk Song
Arr. S. Salz

0928

Go Tell Aunt Rhody

Folk Song
Arr. S. Salz

Go Tell Aunt Rhody

Guitar I

Folk Song
Arr. S. Salz

Go Tell Aunt Rhody

Guitar II

Folk Song
Arr. S. Salz

Go Tell Aunt Rhody

Guitar III

Folk Song
Arr. S. Salz

0928

Go Tell Aunt Rhody

Guitar IV

Folk Song
Arr. S. Salz

Song of the Wind Canon

Folk Song
Arr. S. Salz

0928

Song of the Wind Canon

Guitar I

Folk Song
Arr. S. Salz

Song of the Wind Canon

Guitar II

Folk Song
Arr. S. Salz

0928

Song of the Wind Canon

Guitar III

Folk Song
Arr. S. Salz

Song of the Wind Canon

Guitar IV

Folk Song
Arr. S. Salz

0928

May Song Ensemble

Folk Song
Arr. S. Salz

0928

May Song Ensemble

Folk Song
Arr. S. Salz

May Song Ensemble

Guitar II

Folk Song
Arr. S. Salz

0928

May Song Ensemble

Guitar III

Folk Song
Arr. S. Salz

May Song Ensemble

Guitar IV

Folk Song
Arr. S. Salz

0928

Allegretto Ensemble

S. Suzuki
Arr. S. Salz

0928

Allegretto Ensemble

Guitar I

S. Suzuki
Arr. S. Salz

Allegretto Ensemble

Guitar II

S. Suzuki
Arr. S. Salz

0928

Allegretto Ensemble

Guitar III

S. Suzuki
Arr. S. Salz

Allegretto Ensemble

Guitar IV

S. Suzuki
Arr. S. Salz

0928

Perpetual Motion Ensemble

S. Suzuki
Arr. S. Salz

0928

Perpetual Motion Ensemble

Guitar I

S. Suzuki
Arr. S. Salz

Perpetual Motion Ensemble

Guitar II

S. Suzuki
Arr. S. Salz

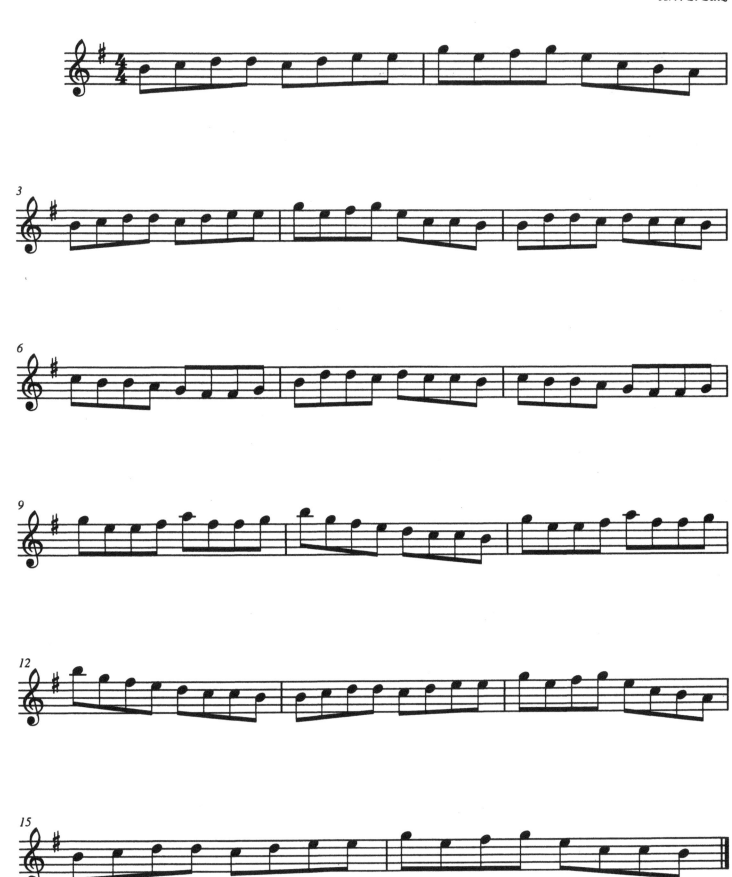

Perpetual Motion Ensemble

Guitar III

S. Suzuki
Arr. S. Salz

0928

Perpetual Motion Ensemble

Guitar IV

S. Suzuki
Arr. S. Salz

sempre sordino